5191 5600

My Math Toolbox

Nancy Kelly Allen

ROURKE
PUBLISHING
www.rourkepublishing.com

www.rourkepublishing.com

PHOTO CREDITS: Cover: © Flashon Studio, Yurchyk, Koratmember; Title Page: © Kone; Page 3: © StHelena, Juriah Mosin; Page 4: © Brooke Fuller, Andrzej Tokarski, Christophe Testi, Andirin; Page 5: © Andrzej Tokarski, Andirin; Page 6: © Andrzej Tokarski, Iperl; Page 7: © Goodynewshoes; Page 8, 21: © Andrzej Tokarski; Page 9: © Andrzej Tokarski, pialhovik; Page 10: © Christophe Testi; Page 11: © Anneke Schram; Page 13: © Eknarin Maphichai; Page 14: © Brooke Fuller; Page 15: © Jordan McCullough; Page 16: © Leian; Page 17: © Leian; Page 18: © Tatyana Nikitina; Page 19: © Andrzej Tokarski, Andirin; Page 22: © Andrzej Tokarski, Tatyana Nikitina, Brooke Fuller, Leian, Iperl; Page 23: © Christophe Testi, Amanda Rohde, Andrzej Tokarski;

Edited by Luana K. Mitten

Cover and Interior design by Teri Intzegian

Library of Congress Cataloging-in-Publication Data

Allen, Nancy Kelly
  My Math Toolbox / Nancy Kelly Allen.
    p. cm. -- (Little World Math)
  Includes bibliographical references and index.
  ISBN 978-1-61741-758-0 (hard cover) (alk. paper)
  ISBN 978-1-61741-960-7 (soft cover)
  Library of Congress Control Number: 2011924823

Rourke Publishing
Printed in the United States of America, North Mankato, Minnesota
060711
060711CL

www.rourkepublishing.com - rourke@rourkepublishing.com
Post Office Box 643328 Vero Beach, Florida 32964

Tools for this, tools for that,
what is in my math toolbox?

My math toolbox is filled with tools I use for math.

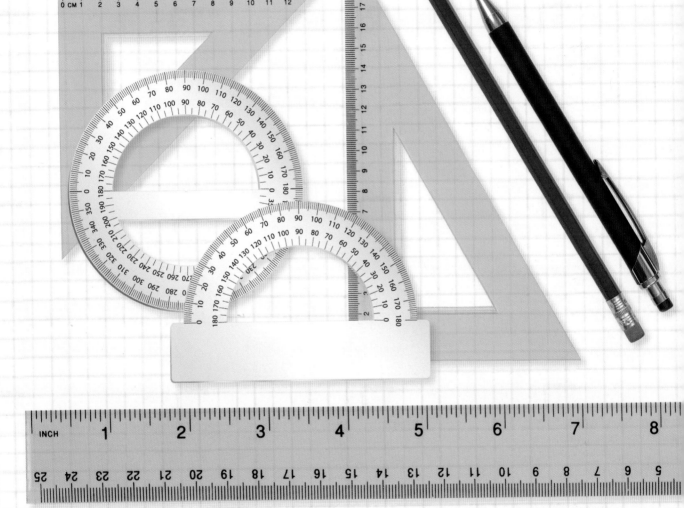

I use my ruler to measure length.

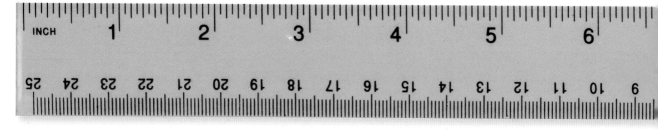

the length of my arm

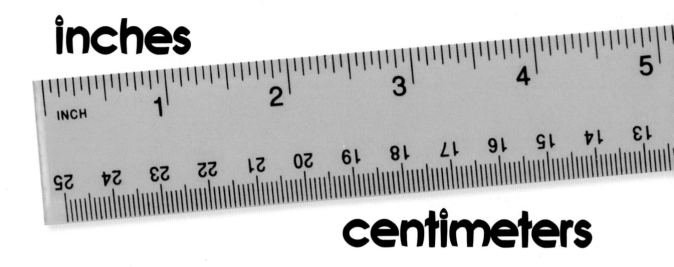

inches

centimeters

My ruler has inches on one side
and centimeters on the other side.

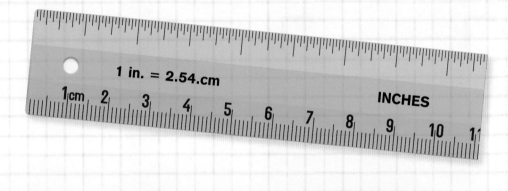

1 in. = 2.54.cm

INCHES

1 cm 2 3 4 5 6 7 8 9 10 11

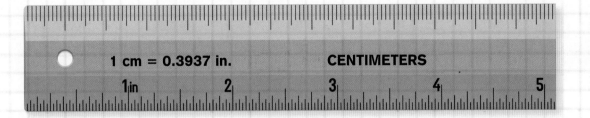

1 cm = 0.3937 in. CENTIMETERS

1 in 2 3 4 5

I use my calculator to add and subtract.

$5 + 3 = ?$

$8 - 2 = ?$

My calculator has buttons with numbers on it.

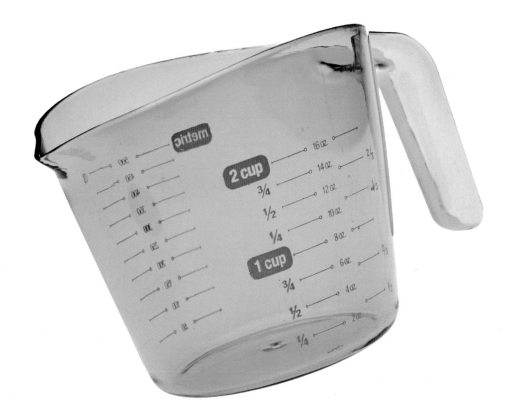

I use my measuring cups to measure
amounts of water and flour.

My measuring cups hold different amounts.

1/2 CUP

1 CUP

1/3 CUP

1/4 CUP

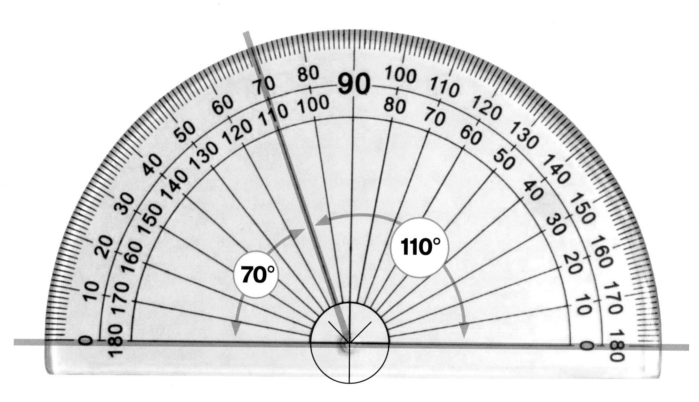

I use my protractor to draw angles.

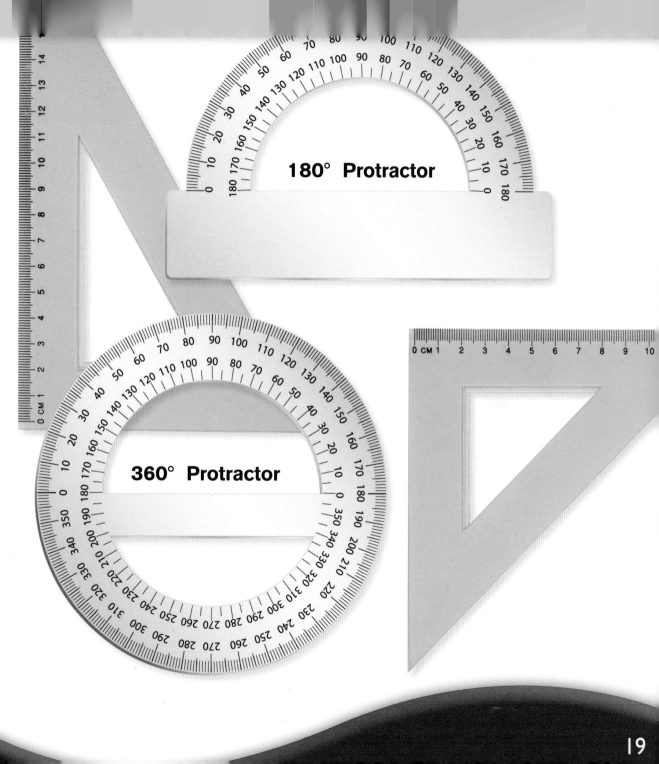

180° Protractor

360° Protractor

My protractor helps
me draw triangles.

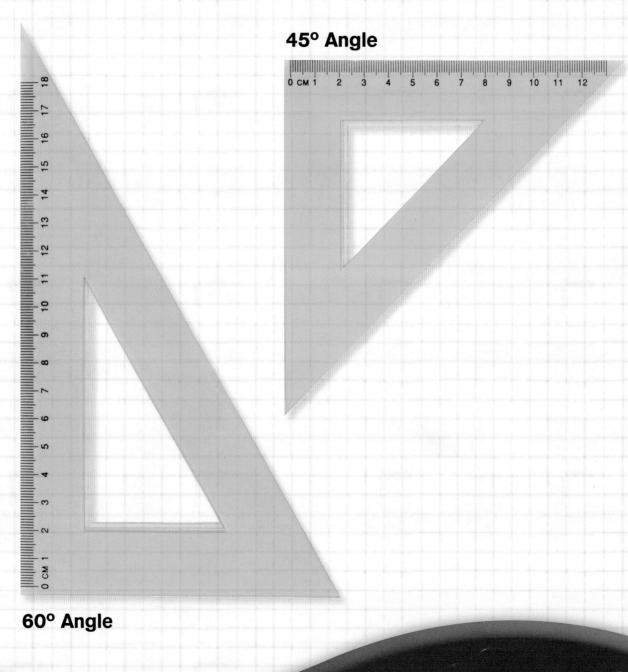

45° Angle

60° Angle

21

Can you match the tool to the job?

$8+9=?$

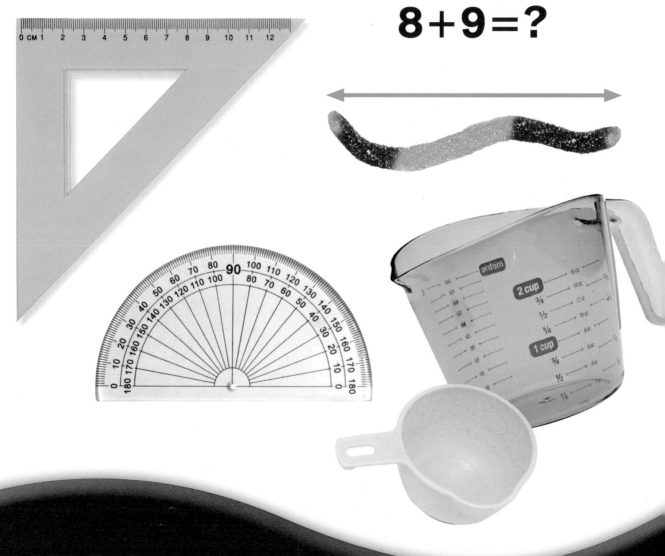

Index

calculator   10, 12

centimeters   8

inches   8

measure   6, 14

protractor   18, 19, 20

ruler   6, 8

tool(s)   3, 4, 22

Websites

www.ixl.com/math/practice/grade-1-adding-zero

www.ixl.com/math/practice/grade-1-subtracting-0

www.prek-8.com/1stgrade/math_adding01.php

www.prek-8.com/1stgrade/math_adding02.php

www.brobstsystems.com/kids/addsheet.htm

About the Author

Nancy Kelly Allen has been writing since she was a little girl. Every day, she opens her writing toolbox. She uses pencils to write, paper to write on, and a calculator to add the number of words. The tool she uses most is a big eraser to get rid of her mistakes.